TABLE OF CONTENTS

This lesson plan book belongs to:

Name _____

School _____

Grade/Subject _____

Room _____

School Year _____

Address _____

Phone _____

Teacher Created Resources, Inc.

12621 Western Avenue
Garden Grove, CA 92841
www.teachercreated.com

ISBN: 978-1-4206-3269-9

©2013 Teacher Created Resources, Inc.
Reprinted, 2020
Made in U.S.A.

Editor in Chief & Creative Director:
Karen Goldfluss, M.S. Ed.

Cover Design: Barb Lorseyedi

Imaging: Ralph Olmedo Jr.

Publisher:
Mary D. Smith, M.S. Ed.

How To Use This Book

Seating Chart (page 3)

A seating chart is provided for easy reference. Table and desk arrangements will vary throughout the year depending on room size, available furniture, grade level taught, teaching style, and academic program needs. To accommodate a variety of classroom arrangements, you may wish to create additional charts and place specific seating information in a separate folder.

Substitute Teacher Information (pages 4 – 5)

Document all pertinent information on these pages. If you have a copy of the layout of your school, attach it to page 5. Otherwise, use the space provided on page 5 to sketch a diagram of the school building and grounds. Be sure to show important locations, such as the office, restrooms, faculty lounge, cafeteria, auditorium, and playground.

Student Roster (pages 6 – 7)

Use the roster to record information for each student. Having the roster in your lesson plan book provides you with quick and easy access to important data for both you and a substitute teacher.

Birthdays (page 8 – 9)

Use these pages to write students' names and birth dates. Recognize each special day with a birthday greeting.

Weekly Schedule (page 10)

If your schedule changes periodically, you may wish to duplicate this page before completing your current schedule. Attach new schedules throughout the year.

Monthly Planners (pages 11 – 16)

In addition to the daily lesson plan pages in this book, we have provided blank calendar pages for year-long planning. They can be used to note special plans, weekly/monthly meetings and appointments, and for other useful information throughout the year. You may wish to reproduce each month, add important information for the class, and then post the calendar months on a bulletin board or other display. Include special events, positive sayings, inspirational quotes, and friendly reminders on each calendar month.

Class Records (pages 17 – 76)

The class record section is designed to provide organized space for recording daily notations or grades for assignments, tests, attendance, tardies, participation, etc. Each page contains a five-week block of spaces so that a student's record for an entire quarter of ten weeks can be read on facing pages. Summary columns for recording total attendance, tardies, and grades appear on the right-hand facing page for each ten-week period.

Lesson Plans (pages 77 – 159)

Use the Daily Lesson Plans section to help you organize your lesson plans each week. There are enough weekly plan pages to cover a 40-week school year. At the top of the left-hand page, fill in the blank to indicate the week dates for which the plans are written. The first column may be used for notes. For special programs requiring more in-depth explanation of plans, reference the specific folder, notebook, guide, etc., to which the teacher should be directed. This is especially helpful to substitute teachers.

Grading Chart (page 160)

A convenient chart for scoring students' work is provided at the back of this book. Use the chart as a quick reference when scoring 3 to 50 items of equal value. To use the chart, simply "connect" the row that matches the total number of items to be scored with the column indicating the number of incorrect items.

By following across the row and up the columns to the intersection point (number), you can determine the raw score. For example, if the total number of items on a given test is 35, and a student marked 5 incorrectly, his or her score would be 86%. The score is obtained by moving across row 35 and up column 5 to the point where they meet (86%).

SEATING ARRANGEMENT IDEAS

The size and shape of your room will play a large part in your seating arrangement.

You may want to change this layout once you are familiar with your students and their needs.

Regardless of your seating plan, the most important concern is that you can easily see all your students and the children in turn have good visibility of you, the board, and other focal points in the room.

1. Basic Row Seating

2. U-Shaped Seating

3. Rectangular Seating

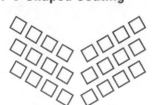

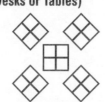

4. V-Shaped Seating

5. Cluster Seating
(Desks or Tables)

6. Partner Seating

Seat Arrangement Floor Plan

Substitute Teacher Information

School Schedule

- Class Begins _____
- Morning Recess _____
- Lunchtime _____
- Class Resumes _____
- Afternoon Recess _____
- Dismissal _____

Special Notes

_____
_____
_____
_____
_____
_____
_____

Special Classes

Student _____

Class _____ Day _____ Time _____

Student _____

Class _____ Day _____ Time _____

Student _____

Class _____ Day _____ Time _____

Where to Find

- Class List _____
- School Layout _____
- Seating Chart _____
- Attendance Record _____
- Lesson Plans _____
- Teacher Manuals _____
- First Aid Kit _____
- Emergency Information _____
- Supplementary Activities _____
- Class Supplies–paper, pencils, etc. _____
- Referral forms and procedures _____

_____
_____
_____
_____
_____
_____
_____
_____
_____
_____
_____
_____

Special Needs Students

Student	Needs	Time and Place
_____	_____	_____
_____	_____	_____
_____	_____	_____
_____	_____	_____
_____	_____	_____

Classroom Guidelines

- When finished with an assignment
  _____
  _____

- When and how to speak out in class
  _____
  _____

- Incentive Program
  _____
  _____

- Discipline
  _____
  _____

- Restroom Procedure
  _____
  _____

People Who Can Help

- Teacher/Room _____
- Dependable Students
  _____
  _____
  _____
  _____

- Principal _____
- Secretary _____
- Custodian _____
- Counselor _____
- Nurse _____

Map of School

Student's Name	Parent's Name	Address
1.		
2		
3.		
4.		
5.		
6.		
7.		
8.		
9.		
10.		
11.		
12.		
13.		
14.		
15.		
16.		
17.		
18.		
19.		
20.		
21.		
22.		
23.		
24.		
25.		
26.		
27.		
28.		
29.		
30.		
31.		
32.		
33.		
34.		
35.		
36.		

ROSTER

Home & Work Phones	Birthday	Siblings	Notes
Home & Work Phones	Birthday	Siblings	Notes

BIRTHDAYS

January

February

March

April

May

June

BIRTHDAYS (cont)

July

August

September

October

November

December

WEEKLY SCHEDULE

Time	Monday	Tuesday	Wednesday	Thursday	Friday

PLANNER

Notes

SUNDAY	MONDAY	TUESDAY	WEDNESDAY	THURSDAY	FRIDAY	SATURDAY

PLANNER

Notes

SUNDAY	MONDAY	TUESDAY	WEDNESDAY	THURSDAY	FRIDAY	SATURDAY

PLANNER

Notes

	SUNDAY	MONDAY	TUESDAY	WEDNESDAY	THURSDAY	FRIDAY	SATURDAY

PLANNER

Notes

	SUNDAY	MONDAY	TUESDAY	WEDNESDAY	THURSDAY	FRIDAY	SATURDAY

PLANNER

Notes

	SUNDAY	MONDAY	TUESDAY	WEDNESDAY	THURSDAY	FRIDAY	SATURDAY

PLANNER

Notes

	SUNDAY	MONDAY	TUESDAY	WEDNESDAY	THURSDAY	FRIDAY	SATURDAY

PLANNER

Notes

	SUNDAY	MONDAY	TUESDAY	WEDNESDAY	THURSDAY	FRIDAY	SATURDAY

PLANNER

Notes

	SUNDAY	MONDAY	TUESDAY	WEDNESDAY	THURSDAY	FRIDAY	SATURDAY

_____ PLANNER

Notes	SUNDAY	MONDAY	TUESDAY	WEDNESDAY	THURSDAY	FRIDAY	SATURDAY

_____ PLANNER

Notes	SUNDAY	MONDAY	TUESDAY	WEDNESDAY	THURSDAY	FRIDAY	SATURDAY

_____ PLANNER

Notes	SUNDAY	MONDAY	TUESDAY	WEDNESDAY	THURSDAY	FRIDAY	SATURDAY

_____ PLANNER

Notes	SUNDAY	MONDAY	TUESDAY	WEDNESDAY	THURSDAY	FRIDAY	SATURDAY

Class Records

	SUBJECT																													
Week	**Week** _____					**Week** _____					**Week** _____					**Week** _____					**Week** _____					**Week** _____				
Day	M	T	W	T	F	M	T	W	T	F	M	T	W	T	F	M	T	W	T	F	M	T	W	T	F	M	T	W	T	F
Date																														
ASSIGNMENTS OR ATTENDANCE																														
Name																														
1																														
2																														
3																														
4																														
5																														
6																														
7																														
8																														
9																														
10																														
11																														
12																														
13																														
14																														
15																														
16																														
17																														
18																														
19																														
20																														
21																														
22																														
23																														
24																														
25																														
26																														
27																														
28																														
29																														
30																														
31																														
32																														
33																														
34																														
35																														
36																														

Period

Week ___				Week ___				Week ___				Week ___				Week ___					DAYS PRESENT	DAYS ABSENT	TARDIES	QUARTER GRADE		
M	T	W	T	F	M	T	W	T	F	M	T	W	T	F	M	T	W	T	F	M	T	W	T	F	
																									1
																									2
																									3
																									4
																									5
																									6
																									7
																									8
																									9
																									10
																									11
																									12
																									13
																									14
																									15
																									16
																									17
																									18
																									19
																									20
																									21
																									22
																									23
																									24
																									25
																									26
																									27
																									28
																									29
																									30
																									31
																									32
																									33
																									34
																									35
																									36

	Week ____	Week ____	Week ____	Week ____	Week ____	Week ____
Week						
Day	M T W T F	M T W T F	M T W T F	M T W T F	M T W T F	M T W T F
Date						
ASSIGNMENTS OR ATTENDANCE						
Name						
1						
2						
3						
4						
5						
6						
7						
8						
9						
10						
11						
12						
13						
14						
15						
16						
17						
18						
19						
20						
21						
22						
23						
24						
25						
26						
27						
28						
29						
30						
31						
32						
33						
34						
35						
36						

Period

Week ____					Week ____					Week ____					Week ____					Week ____						DAYS PRESENT	DAYS ABSENT	TARDIES	QUARTER GRADE	
M	T	W	T	F	M	T	W	T	F	M	T	W	T	F	M	T	W	T	F	M	T	W	T	F					
																									1				
																									2				
																									3				
																									4				
																									5				
																									6				
																									7				
																									8				
																									9				
																									10				
																									11				
																									12				
																									13				
																									14				
																									15				
																									16				
																									17				
																									18				
																									19				
																									20				
																									21				
																									22				
																									23				
																									24				
																									25				
																									26				
																									27				
																									28				
																									29				
																									30				
																									31				
																									32				
																									33				
																									34				
																									35				
																									36				

Week	Week ___					Week ___					Week ___					Week ___					Week ___				
SUBJECT																									
Day	M	T	W	T	F	M	T	W	T	F	M	T	W	T	F	M	T	W	T	F	M	T	W	T	F
Date																									
ASSIGNMENTS OR ATTENDANCE																									
Name																									
1																									
2																									
3																									
4																									
5																									
6																									
7																									
8																									
9																									
10																									
11																									
12																									
13																									
14																									
15																									
16																									
17																									
18																									
19																									
20																									
21																									
22																									
23																									
24																									
25																									
26																									
27																									
28																									
29																									
30																									
31																									
32																									
33																									
34																									
35																									
36																									

Period

Week ___					Week ___					Week ___					Week ___					Week ___						DAYS PRESENT	DAYS ABSENT	TARDIES	QUARTER GRADE	
M	T	W	T	F	M	T	W	T	F	M	T	W	T	F	M	T	W	T	F	M	T	W	T	F						
																									1					
																									2					
																									3					
																									4					
																									5					
																									6					
																									7					
																									8					
																									9					
																									10					
																									11					
																									12					
																									13					
																									14					
																									15					
																									16					
																									17					
																									18					
																									19					
																									20					
																									21					
																									22					
																									23					
																									24					
																									25					
																									26					
																									27					
																									28					
																									29					
																									30					
																									31					
																									32					
																									33					
																									34					
																									35					
																									36					

Week	Week ___					Week ___					Week ___					Week ___					Week ___				
Day	M	T	W	T	F	M	T	W	T	F	M	T	W	T	F	M	T	W	T	F	M	T	W	T	F
Date																									
ASSIGNMENTS OR ATTENDANCE																									
Name																									
1																									
2																									
3																									
4																									
5																									
6																									
7																									
8																									
9																									
10																									
11																									
12																									
13																									
14																									
15																									
16																									
17																									
18																									
19																									
20																									
21																									
22																									
23																									
24																									
25																									
26																									
27																									
28																									
29																									
30																									
31																									
32																									
33																									
34																									
35																									
36																									

SUBJECT

Period

Week ____					Week ____					Week ____					Week ____					Week ____							Days Present	Days Absent	Tardies	Quarter Grade	
M	T	W	T	F	M	T	W	T	F	M	T	W	T	F	M	T	W	T	F	M	T	W	T	F						
																									1					
																									2					
																									3					
																									4					
																									5					
																									6					
																									7					
																									8					
																									9					
																									10					
																									11					
																									12					
																									13					
																									14					
																									15					
																									16					
																									17					
																									18					
																									19					
																									20					
																									21					
																									22					
																									23					
																									24					
																									25					
																									26					
																									27					
																									28					
																									29					
																									30					
																									31					
																									32					
																									33					
																									34					
																									35					
																									36					

Week	Week ____				Week ____				Week ____				Week ____				Week ____			
SUBJECT																				
Day	M	T	W	T	F	M	T	W	T	F	M	T	W	T	F	M	T	W	T	F	M	T	W	T	F
Date																									
ASSIGNMENTS OR ATTENDANCE																									
Name																									
1																									
2																									
3																									
4																									
5																									
6																									
7																									
8																									
9																									
10																									
11																									
12																									
13																									
14																									
15																									
16																									
17																									
18																									
19																									
20																									
21																									
22																									
23																									
24																									
25																									
26																									
27																									
28																									
29																									
30																									
31																									
32																									
33																									
34																									
35																									
36																									

#3269 Lesson Plan and Record Book   26   ©Teacher Created Resources, Inc.

Period

	Week _____	Week _____	Week _____	Week _____	Week _____		DAYS PRESENT	DAYS ABSENT	TARDIES	QUARTER GRADE	
	M T W T F	M T W T F	M T W T F	M T W T F	M T W T F						
1											
2											
3											
4											
5											
6											
7											
8											
9											
10											
11											
12											
13											
14											
15											
16											
17											
18											
19											
20											
21											
22											
23											
24											
25											
26											
27											
28											
29											
30											
31											
32											
33											
34											
35											
36											

	SUBJECT																								
Week	Week _____					Week _____					Week _____					Week _____					Week _____					Week _____
Day	M	T	W	T	F	M	T	W	T	F	M	T	W	T	F	M	T	W	T	F	M	T	W	T	F
Date																									
ASSIGNMENTS OR ATTENDANCE																									
Name																									
1																									
2																									
3																									
4																									
5																									
6																									
7																									
8																									
9																									
10																									
11																									
12																									
13																									
14																									
15																									
16																									
17																									
18																									
19																									
20																									
21																									
22																									
23																									
24																									
25																									
26																									
27																									
28																									
29																									
30																									
31																									
32																									
33																									
34																									
35																									
36																									

Period

Week _____	Week _____	Week _____	Week _____	Week _____		DAYS PRESENT	DAYS ABSENT	TARDIES	QUARTER GRADE	
M T W T F	M T W T F	M T W T F	M T W T F	M T W T F						
					1					
					2					
					3					
					4					
					5					
					6					
					7					
					8					
					9					
					10					
					11					
					12					
					13					
					14					
					15					
					16					
					17					
					18					
					19					
					20					
					21					
					22					
					23					
					24					
					25					
					26					
					27					
					28					
					29					
					30					
					31					
					32					
					33					
					34					
					35					
					36					

Week						Week _____				Week _____				Week _____				Week _____				Week _____
SUBJECT																						
Day		M	T	W	T	F	M	T	W	T	F	M	T	W	T	F	M	T	W	T	F	M	T	W	T	F
Date																						
ASSIGNMENTS OR ATTENDANCE																						
Name																						
1																						
2																						
3																						
4																						
5																						
6																						
7																						
8																						
9																						
10																						
11																						
12																						
13																						
14																						
15																						
16																						
17																						
18																						
19																						
20																						
21																						
22																						
23																						
24																						
25																						
26																						
27																						
28																						
29																						
30																						
31																						
32																						
33																						
34																						
35																						
36																						

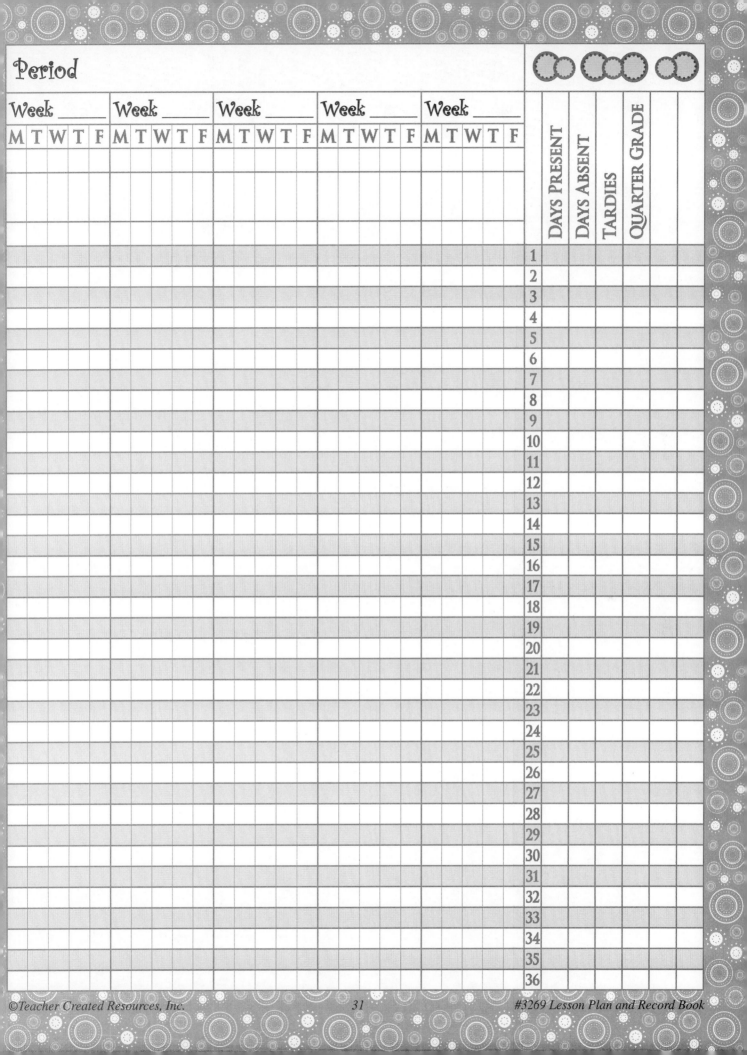

Period																												DAYS PRESENT	DAYS ABSENT	TARDIES	QUARTER GRADE	

Period

Week ____					Week ____					Week ____					Week ____					Week ____						DAYS PRESENT	DAYS ABSENT	TARDIES	QUARTER GRADE	
M	T	W	T	F	M	T	W	T	F	M	T	W	T	F	M	T	W	T	F	M	T	W	T	F						
																									1					
																									2					
																									3					
																									4					
																									5					
																									6					
																									7					
																									8					
																									9					
																									10					
																									11					
																									12					
																									13					
																									14					
																									15					
																									16					
																									17					
																									18					
																									19					
																									20					
																									21					
																									22					
																									23					
																									24					
																									25					
																									26					
																									27					
																									28					
																									29					
																									30					
																									31					
																									32					
																									33					
																									34					
																									35					
																									36					

	Week _____				Week _____				Week _____				Week _____				Week _____			
SUBJECT																				
Week																				
Day	M	T	W	T	F	M	T	W	T	F	M	T	W	T	F	M	T	W	T	F	M	T	W	T	F
Date																				
ASSIGNMENTS OR ATTENDANCE																				
Name																				
1																				
2																				
3																				
4																				
5																				
6																				
7																				
8																				
9																				
10																				
11																				
12																				
13																				
14																				
15																				
16																				
17																				
18																				
19																				
20																				
21																				
22																				
23																				
24																				
25																				
26																				
27																				
28																				
29																				
30																				
31																				
32																				
33																				
34																				
35																				
36																				

Period

Week ____					Week ____					Week ____					Week ____					Week ____						Days Present	Days Absent	Tardies	Quarter Grade	
M	T	W	T	F	M	T	W	T	F	M	T	W	T	F	M	T	W	T	F	M	T	W	T	F					
																									1				
																									2				
																									3				
																									4				
																									5				
																									6				
																									7				
																									8				
																									9				
																									10				
																									11				
																									12				
																									13				
																									14				
																									15				
																									16				
																									17				
																									18				
																									19				
																									20				
																									21				
																									22				
																									23				
																									24				
																									25				
																									26				
																									27				
																									28				
																									29				
																									30				
																									31				
																									32				
																									33				
																									34				
																									35				
																									36				

SUBJECT

Week	Week ___				Week ___				Week ___				Week ___				Week ___			
Day	M	T	W	T	F	M	T	W	T	F	M	T	W	T	F	M	T	W	T	F	M	T	W	T	F
Date																									
ASSIGNMENTS OR ATTENDANCE																									
Name																									
1																									
2																									
3																									
4																									
5																									
6																									
7																									
8																									
9																									
10																									
11																									
12																									
13																									
14																									
15																									
16																									
17																									
18																									
19																									
20																									
21																									
22																									
23																									
24																									
25																									
26																									
27																									
28																									
29																									
30																									
31																									
32																									
33																									
34																									
35																									
36																									

Period

	Week _____	Week _____	Week _____	Week _____	Week _____		DAYS PRESENT	DAYS ABSENT	TARDIES	QUARTER GRADE	
	M T W T F	M T W T F	M T W T F	M T W T F	M T W T F						
						1					
						2					
						3					
						4					
						5					
						6					
						7					
						8					
						9					
						10					
						11					
						12					
						13					
						14					
						15					
						16					
						17					
						18					
						19					
						20					
						21					
						22					
						23					
						24					
						25					
						26					
						27					
						28					
						29					
						30					
						31					
						32					
						33					
						34					
						35					
						36					

SUBJECT

Week	Week ____				Week ____				Week ____				Week ____				Week ____			
Day	M	T	W	T	F	M	T	W	T	F	M	T	W	T	F	M	T	W	T	F	M	T	W	T	F
Date																									
ASSIGNMENTS OR ATTENDANCE																									
Name																									
1																									
2																									
3																									
4																									
5																									
6																									
7																									
8																									
9																									
10																									
11																									
12																									
13																									
14																									
15																									
16																									
17																									
18																									
19																									
20																									
21																									
22																									
23																									
24																									
25																									
26																									
27																									
28																									
29																									
30																									
31																									
32																									
33																									
34																									
35																									
36																									

Period

Week ____					Week ____					Week ____					Week ____					Week ____						DAYS PRESENT	DAYS ABSENT	TARDIES	QUARTER GRADE	
M	T	W	T	F	M	T	W	T	F	M	T	W	T	F	M	T	W	T	F	M	T	W	T	F						
																									1					
																									2					
																									3					
																									4					
																									5					
																									6					
																									7					
																									8					
																									9					
																									10					
																									11					
																									12					
																									13					
																									14					
																									15					
																									16					
																									17					
																									18					
																									19					
																									20					
																									21					
																									22					
																									23					
																									24					
																									25					
																									26					
																									27					
																									28					
																									29					
																									30					
																									31					
																									32					
																									33					
																									34					
																									35					
																									36					

		Week ____				Week ____				Week ____				Week ____				Week ____				Week ____			

SUBJECT

Week Day Date ASSIGNMENTS OR ATTENDANCE Name		M	T	W	T	F	M	T	W	T	F	M	T	W	T	F	M	T	W	T	F	M	T	W	T	F	M	T	W	T	F
	1																														
	2																														
	3																														
	4																														
	5																														
	6																														
	7																														
	8																														
	9																														
	10																														
	11																														
	12																														
	13																														
	14																														
	15																														
	16																														
	17																														
	18																														
	19																														
	20																														
	21																														
	22																														
	23																														
	24																														
	25																														
	26																														
	27																														
	28																														
	29																														
	30																														
	31																														
	32																														
	33																														
	34																														
	35																														
	36																														

Period

Week ____	Week ____	Week ____	Week ____	Week ____		DAYS PRESENT	DAYS ABSENT	TARDIES	QUARTER GRADE	
M T W T F	M T W T F	M T W T F	M T W T F	M T W T F						
					1					
					2					
					3					
					4					
					5					
					6					
					7					
					8					
					9					
					10					
					11					
					12					
					13					
					14					
					15					
					16					
					17					
					18					
					19					
					20					
					21					
					22					
					23					
					24					
					25					
					26					
					27					
					28					
					29					
					30					
					31					
					32					
					33					
					34					
					35					
					36					

Week	Week _____				Week _____				Week _____				Week _____				Week _____				Week _____			
SUBJECT																								
Day	M	T	W	T	F	M	T	W	T	F	M	T	W	T	F	M	T	W	T	F	M	T	W	T	F
Date																									
ASSIGNMENTS OR ATTENDANCE																									
Name																									
1																									
2																									
3																									
4																									
5																									
6																									
7																									
8																									
9																									
10																									
11																									
12																									
13																									
14																									
15																									
16																									
17																									
18																									
19																									
20																									
21																									
22																									
23																									
24																									
25																									
26																									
27																									
28																									
29																									
30																									
31																									
32																									
33																									
34																									
35																									
36																									

Period

Week _____					Week _____					Week _____					Week _____					Week _____						DAYS PRESENT	DAYS ABSENT	TARDIES	QUARTER GRADE	
M	T	W	T	F	M	T	W	T	F	M	T	W	T	F	M	T	W	T	F	M	T	W	T	F						
																									1					
																									2					
																									3					
																									4					
																									5					
																									6					
																									7					
																									8					
																									9					
																									10					
																									11					
																									12					
																									13					
																									14					
																									15					
																									16					
																									17					
																									18					
																									19					
																									20					
																									21					
																									22					
																									23					
																									24					
																									25					
																									26					
																									27					
																									28					
																									29					
																									30					
																									31					
																									32					
																									33					
																									34					
																									35					
																									36					

SUBJECT	Week ___				Week ___				Week ___				Week ___				Week ___				Week ___			
Week																								
Day	M	T	W	T	F	M	T	W	T	F	M	T	W	T	F	M	T	W	T	F	M	T	W	T	F
Date																									
ASSIGNMENTS OR ATTENDANCE																									
Name																									
1																									
2																									
3																									
4																									
5																									
6																									
7																									
8																									
9																									
10																									
11																									
12																									
13																									
14																									
15																									
16																									
17																									
18																									
19																									
20																									
21																									
22																									
23																									
24																									
25																									
26																									
27																									
28																									
29																									
30																									
31																									
32																									
33																									
34																									
35																									
36																									

Period

Week ____					Week ____					Week ____					Week ____					Week ____						DAYS PRESENT	DAYS ABSENT	TARDIES	QUARTER GRADE	
M	T	W	T	F	M	T	W	T	F	M	T	W	T	F	M	T	W	T	F	M	T	W	T	F						
																									1					
																									2					
																									3					
																									4					
																									5					
																									6					
																									7					
																									8					
																									9					
																									10					
																									11					
																									12					
																									13					
																									14					
																									15					
																									16					
																									17					
																									18					
																									19					
																									20					
																									21					
																									22					
																									23					
																									24					
																									25					
																									26					
																									27					
																									28					
																									29					
																									30					
																									31					
																									32					
																									33					
																									34					
																									35					
																									36					

SUBJECT

Week	Week _____				Week _____				Week _____				Week _____				Week _____			
Day	M	T	W	T	F	M	T	W	T	F	M	T	W	T	F	M	T	W	T	F
Date																				
ASSIGNMENTS OR ATTENDANCE																				
Name																				
1																				
2																				
3																				
4																				
5																				
6																				
7																				
8																				
9																				
10																				
11																				
12																				
13																				
14																				
15																				
16																				
17																				
18																				
19																				
20																				
21																				
22																				
23																				
24																				
25																				
26																				
27																				
28																				
29																				
30																				
31																				
32																				
33																				
34																				
35																				
36																				

Period

Week _____					Week _____					Week _____					Week _____					Week _____						DAYS PRESENT	DAYS ABSENT	TARDIES	QUARTER GRADE	
M	T	W	T	F	M	T	W	T	F	M	T	W	T	F	M	T	W	T	F	M	T	W	T	F						
																									1					
																									2					
																									3					
																									4					
																									5					
																									6					
																									7					
																									8					
																									9					
																									10					
																									11					
																									12					
																									13					
																									14					
																									15					
																									16					
																									17					
																									18					
																									19					
																									20					
																									21					
																									22					
																									23					
																									24					
																									25					
																									26					
																									27					
																									28					
																									29					
																									30					
																									31					
																									32					
																									33					
																									34					
																									35					
																									36					

	SUBJECT																								
Week	Week ____					Week ____					Week ____					Week ____					Week ____				
Day	M	T	W	T	F	M	T	W	T	F	M	T	W	T	F	M	T	W	T	F	M	T	W	T	F
Date																									
ASSIGNMENTS OR ATTENDANCE																									
Name																									
1																									
2																									
3																									
4																									
5																									
6																									
7																									
8																									
9																									
10																									
11																									
12																									
13																									
14																									
15																									
16																									
17																									
18																									
19																									
20																									
21																									
22																									
23																									
24																									
25																									
26																									
27																									
28																									
29																									
30																									
31																									
32																									
33																									
34																									
35																									
36																									

Period

Week ____					Week ____					Week ____					Week ____					Week ____						DAYS PRESENT	DAYS ABSENT	TARDIES	QUARTER GRADE	
M	T	W	T	F	M	T	W	T	F	M	T	W	T	F	M	T	W	T	F	M	T	W	T	F						
																									1					
																									2					
																									3					
																									4					
																									5					
																									6					
																									7					
																									8					
																									9					
																									10					
																									11					
																									12					
																									13					
																									14					
																									15					
																									16					
																									17					
																									18					
																									19					
																									20					
																									21					
																									22					
																									23					
																									24					
																									25					
																									26					
																									27					
																									28					
																									29					
																									30					
																									31					
																									32					
																									33					
																									34					
																									35					
																									36					

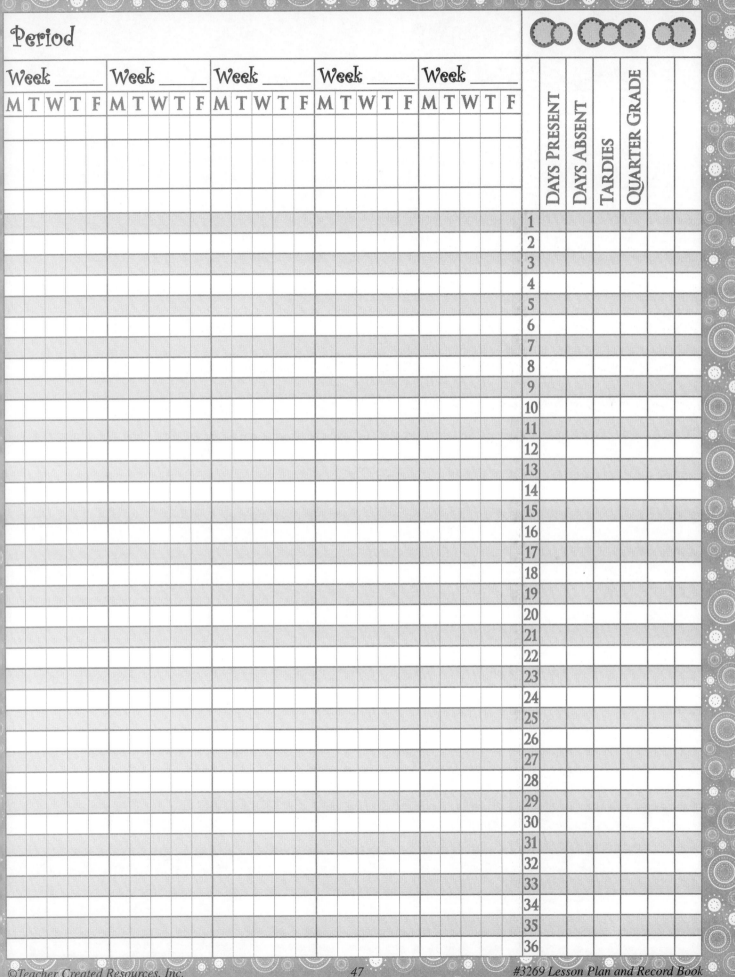

	SUBJECT																								
Week	Week _____					Week _____					Week _____					Week _____					Week _____				
Day	M	T	W	T	F	M	T	W	T	F	M	T	W	T	F	M	T	W	T	F	M	T	W	T	F
Date																									
ASSIGNMENTS OR ATTENDANCE																									
Name																									
1																									
2																									
3																									
4																									
5																									
6																									
7																									
8																									
9																									
10																									
11																									
12																									
13																									
14																									
15																									
16																									
17																									
18																									
19																									
20																									
21																									
22																									
23																									
24																									
25																									
26																									
27																									
28																									
29																									
30																									
31																									
32																									
33																									
34																									
35																									
36																									

Period

| Week _____ | Week _____ | Week _____ | Week _____ | Week _____ | | DAYS PRESENT | DAYS ABSENT | TARDIES | QUARTER GRADE | |
M	T	W	T	F	M	T	W	T	F	M	T	W	T	F	M	T	W	T	F	M	T	W	T	F						
																									1					
																									2					
																									3					
																									4					
																									5					
																									6					
																									7					
																									8					
																									9					
																									10					
																									11					
																									12					
																									13					
																									14					
																									15					
																									16					
																									17					
																									18					
																									19					
																									20					
																									21					
																									22					
																									23					
																									24					
																									25					
																									26					
																									27					
																									28					
																									29					
																									30					
																									31					
																									32					
																									33					
																									34					
																									35					
																									36					

	SUBJECT					Week ____				Week ____				Week ____				Week ____				Week ____	
Week					Week ____																		
Day	M	T	W	T	F	M	T	W	T	F	M	T	W	T	F	M	T	W	T	F	M	T	W	T	F
Date																								
ASSIGNMENTS OR ATTENDANCE																								
Name																								
1																								
2																								
3																								
4																								
5																								
6																								
7																								
8																								
9																								
10																								
11																								
12																								
13																								
14																								
15																								
16																								
17																								
18																								
19																								
20																								
21																								
22																								
23																								
24																								
25																								
26																								
27																								
28																								
29																								
30																								
31																								
32																								
33																								
34																								
35																								
36																								

Period

Week _____				Week _____				Week _____				Week _____				Week _____						DAYS PRESENT	DAYS ABSENT	TARDIES	QUARTER GRADE	
M	T	W	T	F	M	T	W	T	F	M	T	W	T	F	M	T	W	T	F	M	T	W	T	F						
																									1					
																									2					
																									3					
																									4					
																									5					
																									6					
																									7					
																									8					
																									9					
																									10					
																									11					
																									12					
																									13					
																									14					
																									15					
																									16					
																									17					
																									18					
																									19					
																									20					
																									21					
																									22					
																									23					
																									24					
																									25					
																									26					
																									27					
																									28					
																									29					
																									30					
																									31					
																									32					
																									33					
																									34					
																									35					
																									36					

	SUBJECT																													
Week	Week _____					Week _____					Week _____					Week _____					Week _____					Week _____				
Day	M	T	W	T	F	M	T	W	T	F	M	T	W	T	F	M	T	W	T	F	M	T	W	T	F	M	T	W	T	F
Date																														
ASSIGNMENTS OR ATTENDANCE																														
Name																														
1																														
2																														
3																														
4																														
5																														
6																														
7																														
8																														
9																														
10																														
11																														
12																														
13																														
14																														
15																														
16																														
17																														
18																														
19																														
20																														
21																														
22																														
23																														
24																														
25																														
26																														
27																														
28																														
29																														
30																														
31																														
32																														
33																														
34																														
35																														
36																														

Period

Week _____					Week _____					Week _____					Week _____					Week _____						DAYS PRESENT	DAYS ABSENT	TARDIES	QUARTER GRADE	
M	T	W	T	F	M	T	W	T	F	M	T	W	T	F	M	T	W	T	F	M	T	W	T	F						
																									1					
																									2					
																									3					
																									4					
																									5					
																									6					
																									7					
																									8					
																									9					
																									10					
																									11					
																									12					
																									13					
																									14					
																									15					
																									16					
																									17					
																									18					
																									19					
																									20					
																									21					
																									22					
																									23					
																									24					
																									25					
																									26					
																									27					
																									28					
																									29					
																									30					
																									31					
																									32					
																									33					
																									34					
																									35					
																									36					

Period

©Teacher Created Resources, Inc.   53   #3269 Lesson Plan and Record Book

 **SUBJECT**

Week	Week _____				Week _____				Week _____				Week _____				Week _____				Week _____			
Day	M	T	W	T	F	M	T	W	T	F	M	T	W	T	F	M	T	W	T	F	M	T	W	T	F
Date																									
ASSIGNMENTS OR ATTENDANCE																									
Name																									
1																									
2																									
3																									
4																									
5																									
6																									
7																									
8																									
9																									
10																									
11																									
12																									
13																									
14																									
15																									
16																									
17																									
18																									
19																									
20																									
21																									
22																									
23																									
24																									
25																									
26																									
27																									
28																									
29																									
30																									
31																									
32																									
33																									
34																									
35																									
36																									

Period

Week ____	Week ____	Week ____	Week ____	Week ____		DAYS PRESENT	DAYS ABSENT	TARDIES	QUARTER GRADE	
M T W T F	M T W T F	M T W T F	M T W T F	M T W T F						
					1					
					2					
					3					
					4					
					5					
					6					
					7					
					8					
					9					
					10					
					11					
					12					
					13					
					14					
					15					
					16					
					17					
					18					
					19					
					20					
					21					
					22					
					23					
					24					
					25					
					26					
					27					
					28					
					29					
					30					
					31					
					32					
					33					
					34					
					35					
					36					

Week	SUBJECT																											
Week	Week ____				Week ____				Week ____				Week ____				Week ____				Week ____							
Day	M	T	W	T	F	M	T	W	T	F	M	T	W	T	F	M	T	W	T	F	M	T	W	T	F	M	T	W	T	F
Date																														
ASSIGNMENTS OR ATTENDANCE																														
Name																														
1																														
2																														
3																														
4																														
5																														
6																														
7																														
8																														
9																														
10																														
11																														
12																														
13																														
14																														
15																														
16																														
17																														
18																														
19																														
20																														
21																														
22																														
23																														
24																														
25																														
26																														
27																														
28																														
29																														
30																														
31																														
32																														
33																														
34																														
35																														
36																														

Period

Week ___					Week ___					Week ___					Week ___					Week ___						DAYS PRESENT	DAYS ABSENT	TARDIES	QUARTER GRADE	
M	T	W	T	F	M	T	W	T	F	M	T	W	T	F	M	T	W	T	F	M	T	W	T	F						
																									1					
																									2					
																									3					
																									4					
																									5					
																									6					
																									7					
																									8					
																									9					
																									10					
																									11					
																									12					
																									13					
																									14					
																									15					
																									16					
																									17					
																									18					
																									19					
																									20					
																									21					
																									22					
																									23					
																									24					
																									25					
																									26					
																									27					
																									28					
																									29					
																									30					
																									31					
																									32					
																									33					
																									34					
																									35					
																									36					

	SUBJECT					Week ____					Week ____					Week ____					Week ____					Week ____				
Week																													
Day	M	T	W	T	F	M	T	W	T	F	M	T	W	T	F	M	T	W	T	F	M	T	W	T	F	M	T	W	T	F
Date																														
ASSIGNMENTS OR ATTENDANCE																														
Name																														
1																														
2																														
3																														
4																														
5																														
6																														
7																														
8																														
9																														
10																														
11																														
12																														
13																														
14																														
15																														
16																														
17																														
18																														
19																														
20																														
21																														
22																														
23																														
24																														
25																														
26																														
27																														
28																														
29																														
30																														
31																														
32																														
33																														
34																														
35																														
36																														

Period

Week ____	Week ____	Week ____	Week ____	Week ____		DAYS PRESENT	DAYS ABSENT	TARDIES	QUARTER GRADE		
M T W T F	M T W T F	M T W T F	M T W T F	M T W T F							
					1						
					2						
					3						
					4						
					5						
					6						
					7						
					8						
					9						
					10						
					11						
					12						
					13						
					14						
					15						
					16						
					17						
					18						
					19						
					20						
					21						
					22						
					23						
					24						
					25						
					26						
					27						
					28						
					29						
					30						
					31						
					32						
					33						
					34						
					35						
					36						

SUBJECT

Week	Week ___				Week ___				Week ___				Week ___				Week ___		
Day	M	T	W	T	F	M	T	W	T	F	M	T	W	T	F	M	T	W	T	F	M	T	W	T	F
Date																									
ASSIGNMENTS OR ATTENDANCE																									
Name																									
1																									
2																									
3																									
4																									
5																									
6																									
7																									
8																									
9																									
10																									
11																									
12																									
13																									
14																									
15																									
16																									
17																									
18																									
19																									
20																									
21																									
22																									
23																									
24																									
25																									
26																									
27																									
28																									
29																									
30																									
31																									
32																									
33																									
34																									
35																									
36																									

Period

																										DAYS PRESENT	DAYS ABSENT	TARDIES	QUARTER GRADE	
Week ____				Week ____				Week ____				Week ____				Week ____														
M	T	W	T	F	M	T	W	T	F	M	T	W	T	F	M	T	W	T	F	M	T	W	T	F	1					
																									2					
																									3					
																									4					
																									5					
																									6					
																									7					
																									8					
																									9					
																									10					
																									11					
																									12					
																									13					
																									14					
																									15					
																									16					
																									17					
																									18					
																									19					
																									20					
																									21					
																									22					
																									23					
																									24					
																									25					
																									26					
																									27					
																									28					
																									29					
																									30					
																									31					
																									32					
																									33					
																									34					
																									35					
																									36					

	SUBJECT				Week _____					Week _____					Week _____					Week _____					Week _____				Week _____
Week					**Week** _____					**Week** _____					**Week** _____					**Week** _____					**Week** _____					**Week** _____
Day					M	T	W	T	F	M	T	W	T	F	M	T	W	T	F	M	T	W	T	F	M	T	W	T	F	M	T	W	T	F
Date																																		
ASSIGNMENTS OR ATTENDANCE																																		
Name																																		
1																																		
2																																		
3																																		
4																																		
5																																		
6																																		
7																																		
8																																		
9																																		
10																																		
11																																		
12																																		
13																																		
14																																		
15																																		
16																																		
17																																		
18																																		
19																																		
20																																		
21																																		
22																																		
23																																		
24																																		
25																																		
26																																		
27																																		
28																																		
29																																		
30																																		
31																																		
32																																		
33																																		
34																																		
35																																		
36																																		

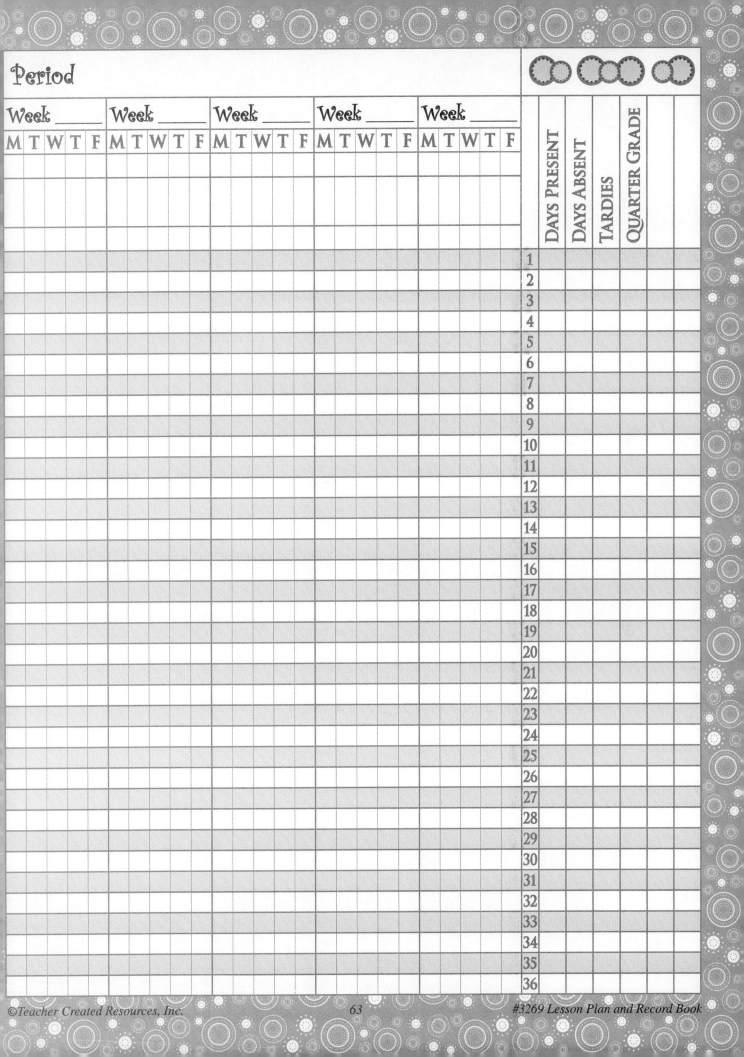

Period

Week ___					Week ___					Week ___					Week ___					Week ___						DAYS PRESENT	DAYS ABSENT	TARDIES	QUARTER GRADE	
M	T	W	T	F	M	T	W	T	F	M	T	W	T	F	M	T	W	T	F	M	T	W	T	F						
																									1					
																									2					
																									3					
																									4					
																									5					
																									6					
																									7					
																									8					
																									9					
																									10					
																									11					
																									12					
																									13					
																									14					
																									15					
																									16					
																									17					
																									18					
																									19					
																									20					
																									21					
																									22					
																									23					
																									24					
																									25					
																									26					
																									27					
																									28					
																									29					
																									30					
																									31					
																									32					
																									33					
																									34					
																									35					
																									36					

	SUBJECT																														
Week	Week ____				Week ____				Week ____				Week ____				Week ____				Week ____			
Day	M	T	W	T	F	M	T	W	T	F	M	T	W	T	F	M	T	W	T	F	M	T	W	T	F	M	T	W	T	F
Date																														
ASSIGNMENTS OR ATTENDANCE																														
Name																														
1																														
2																														
3																														
4																														
5																														
6																														
7																														
8																														
9																														
10																														
11																														
12																														
13																														
14																														
15																														
16																														
17																														
18																														
19																														
20																														
21																														
22																														
23																														
24																														
25																														
26																														
27																														
28																														
29																														
30																														
31																														
32																														
33																														
34																														
35																														
36																														

Period

Week ____					Week ____					Week ____					Week ____					Week ____						DAYS PRESENT	DAYS ABSENT	TARDIES	QUARTER GRADE	
M	T	W	T	F	M	T	W	T	F	M	T	W	T	F	M	T	W	T	F	M	T	W	T	F						
																									1					
																									2					
																									3					
																									4					
																									5					
																									6					
																									7					
																									8					
																									9					
																									10					
																									11					
																									12					
																									13					
																									14					
																									15					
																									16					
																									17					
																									18					
																									19					
																									20					
																									21					
																									22					
																									23					
																									24					
																									25					
																									26					
																									27					
																									28					
																									29					
																									30					
																									31					
																									32					
																									33					
																									34					
																									35					
																									36					

	SUBJECT					Week _____				Week _____				Week _____				Week _____				Week _____				Week _____			
Week																												
Day						M	T	W	T	F	M	T	W	T	F	M	T	W	T	F	M	T	W	T	F	M	T	W	T	F
Date																															
ASSIGNMENTS OR ATTENDANCE																															
Name																															
1																															
2																															
3																															
4																															
5																															
6																															
7																															
8																															
9																															
10																															
11																															
12																															
13																															
14																															
15																															
16																															
17																															
18																															
19																															
20																															
21																															
22																															
23																															
24																															
25																															
26																															
27																															
28																															
29																															
30																															
31																															
32																															
33																															
34																															
35																															
36																															

Period

Week ___				Week ___				Week ___				Week ___				Week ___					DAYS PRESENT	DAYS ABSENT	TARDIES	QUARTER GRADE	
M	T	W	T	F	M	T	W	T	F	M	T	W	T	F	M	T	W	T	F	M	T	W	T	F						
																									1					
																									2					
																									3					
																									4					
																									5					
																									6					
																									7					
																									8					
																									9					
																									10					
																									11					
																									12					
																									13					
																									14					
																									15					
																									16					
																									17					
																									18					
																									19					
																									20					
																									21					
																									22					
																									23					
																									24					
																									25					
																									26					
																									27					
																									28					
																									29					
																									30					
																									31					
																									32					
																									33					
																									34					
																									35					
																									36					

	SUBJECT																														
Week	Week ____					Week ____					Week ____					Week ____					Week ____					Week ____				
Day	M	T	W	T	F	M	T	W	T	F	M	T	W	T	F	M	T	W	T	F	M	T	W	T	F	M	T	W	T	F
Date																														
ASSIGNMENTS OR ATTENDANCE																														
Name																														
1																														
2																														
3																														
4																														
5																														
6																														
7																														
8																														
9																														
10																														
11																														
12																														
13																														
14																														
15																														
16																														
17																														
18																														
19																														
20																														
21																														
22																														
23																														
24																														
25																														
26																														
27																														
28																														
29																														
30																														
31																														
32																														
33																														
34																														
35																														
36																														

Period

	Week ____				Week ____				Week ____				Week ____				Week ____						DAYS PRESENT	DAYS ABSENT	TARDIES	QUARTER GRADE	
M	T	W	T	F	M	T	W	T	F	M	T	W	T	F	M	T	W	T	F	M	T	W	T	F						
																									1					
																									2					
																									3					
																									4					
																									5					
																									6					
																									7					
																									8					
																									9					
																									10					
																									11					
																									12					
																									13					
																									14					
																									15					
																									16					
																									17					
																									18					
																									19					
																									20					
																									21					
																									22					
																									23					
																									24					
																									25					
																									26					
																									27					
																									28					
																									29					
																									30					
																									31					
																									32					
																									33					
																									34					
																									35					
																									36					

SUBJECT

Week	Week _____					Week _____					Week _____					Week _____					Week _____					Week _____				
Day	M	T	W	T	F	M	T	W	T	F	M	T	W	T	F	M	T	W	T	F	M	T	W	T	F	M	T	W	T	F
Date																														
ASSIGNMENTS OR ATTENDANCE																														
Name																														
1																														
2																														
3																														
4																														
5																														
6																														
7																														
8																														
9																														
10																														
11																														
12																														
13																														
14																														
15																														
16																														
17																														
18																														
19																														
20																														
21																														
22																														
23																														
24																														
25																														
26																														
27																														
28																														
29																														
30																														
31																														
32																														
33																														
34																														
35																														
36																														

Period

Week ___	Week ___	Week ___	Week ___	Week ___		DAYS PRESENT	DAYS ABSENT	TARDIES	QUARTER GRADE	
M T W T F	M T W T F	M T W T F	M T W T F	M T W T F						
					1					
					2					
					3					
					4					
					5					
					6					
					7					
					8					
					9					
					10					
					11					
					12					
					13					
					14					
					15					
					16					
					17					
					18					
					19					
					20					
					21					
					22					
					23					
					24					
					25					
					26					
					27					
					28					
					29					
					30					
					31					
					32					
					33					
					34					
					35					
					36					

	SUBJECT	Week ____	Week ____	Week ____	Week ____	Week ____
Week		M T W T F	M T W T F	M T W T F	M T W T F	M T W T F
Day						
Date						
ASSIGNMENTS OR ATTENDANCE						
Name						
	1					
	2					
	3					
	4					
	5					
	6					
	7					
	8					
	9					
	10					
	11					
	12					
	13					
	14					
	15					
	16					
	17					
	18					
	19					
	20					
	21					
	22					
	23					
	24					
	25					
	26					
	27					
	28					
	29					
	30					
	31					
	32					
	33					
	34					
	35					
	36					

Period

Week ___					Week ___					Week ___					Week ___					Week ___						DAYS PRESENT	DAYS ABSENT	TARDIES	QUARTER GRADE	
M	T	W	T	F	M	T	W	T	F	M	T	W	T	F	M	T	W	T	F	M	T	W	T	F						
																									1					
																									2					
																									3					
																									4					
																									5					
																									6					
																									7					
																									8					
																									9					
																									10					
																									11					
																									12					
																									13					
																									14					
																									15					
																									16					
																									17					
																									18					
																									19					
																									20					
																									21					
																									22					
																									23					
																									24					
																									25					
																									26					
																									27					
																									28					
																									29					
																									30					
																									31					
																									32					
																									33					
																									34					
																									35					
																									36					

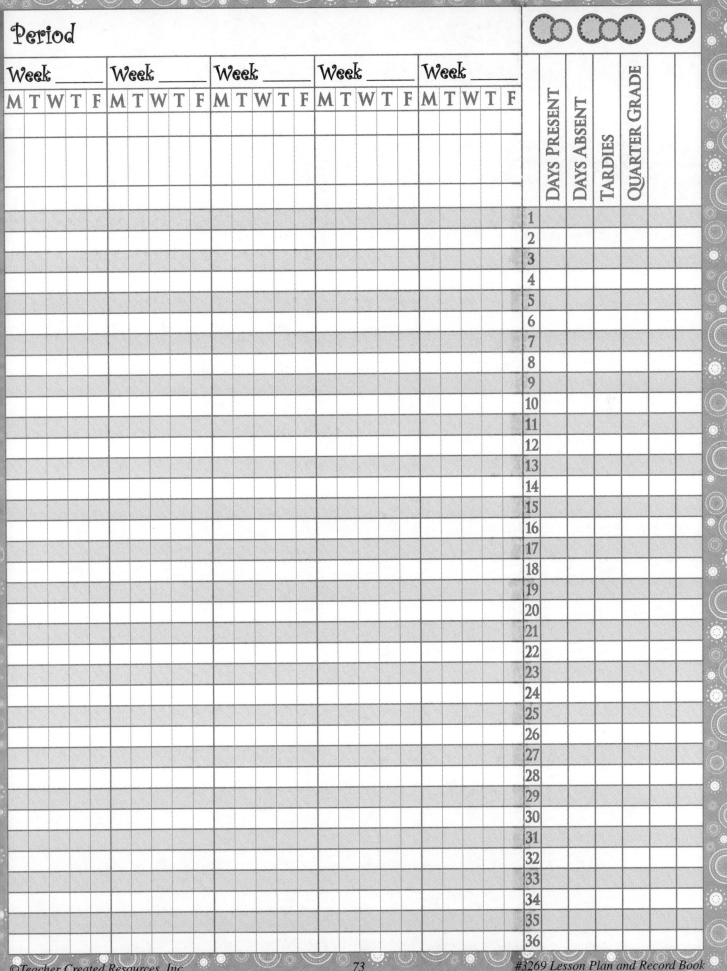

Week	Week _____				Week _____				Week _____				Week _____				Week _____				Week _____			
SUBJECT																								
Day	M	T	W	T	F	M	T	W	T	F	M	T	W	T	F	M	T	W	T	F	M	T	W	T	F
Date																									
ASSIGNMENTS OR ATTENDANCE																									
Name																									
1																									
2																									
3																									
4																									
5																									
6																									
7																									
8																									
9																									
10																									
11																									
12																									
13																									
14																									
15																									
16																									
17																									
18																									
19																									
20																									
21																									
22																									
23																									
24																									
25																									
26																									
27																									
28																									
29																									
30																									
31																									
32																									
33																									
34																									
35																									
36																									

Period

Week ___	Week ___	Week ___	Week ___	Week ___		DAYS PRESENT	DAYS ABSENT	TARDIES	QUARTER GRADE	
M T W T F	M T W T F	M T W T F	M T W T F	M T W T F						
					1					
					2					
					3					
					4					
					5					
					6					
					7					
					8					
					9					
					10					
					11					
					12					
					13					
					14					
					15					
					16					
					17					
					18					
					19					
					20					
					21					
					22					
					23					
					24					
					25					
					26					
					27					
					28					
					29					
					30					
					31					
					32					
					33					
					34					
					35					
					36					

NOTES

Lesson Plans

Notes	MONDAY	TUESDAY

WEDNESDAY	THURSDAY	FRIDAY

WEEK OF

Notes	MONDAY	TUESDAY

WEDNESDAY	THURSDAY	FRIDAY

Notes	MONDAY	TUESDAY

82

WEDNESDAY	THURSDAY	FRIDAY

Notes	MONDAY	TUESDAY

WEDNESDAY	THURSDAY	FRIDAY

Notes

MONDAY

TUESDAY

WEDNESDAY	THURSDAY	FRIDAY

WEEK OF

Notes

MONDAY

TUESDAY

WEDNESDAY	THURSDAY	FRIDAY

Notes	MONDAY	TUESDAY

WEDNESDAY	THURSDAY	FRIDAY

Notes

MONDAY

TUESDAY

WEDNESDAY	THURSDAY	FRIDAY

Notes	MONDAY	TUESDAY

WEDNESDAY	THURSDAY	FRIDAY

Notes

MONDAY

TUESDAY

WEDNESDAY	THURSDAY	FRIDAY

Notes	MONDAY	TUESDAY

WEDNESDAY	THURSDAY	FRIDAY

WEEK OF

Notes	MONDAY	TUESDAY

WEDNESDAY	THURSDAY	FRIDAY

Notes	MONDAY	TUESDAY

WEDNESDAY	THURSDAY	FRIDAY

WEEK OF

Notes	MONDAY	TUESDAY

WEDNESDAY	THURSDAY	FRIDAY

Notes

MONDAY

TUESDAY

WEDNESDAY	THURSDAY	FRIDAY

⦾⦾ Notes ⦾⦾	MONDAY	TUESDAY

WEDNESDAY	THURSDAY	FRIDAY

WEEK OF

Notes	MONDAY	TUESDAY

WEDNESDAY

THURSDAY

FRIDAY

WEEK OF

Notes	MONDAY	TUESDAY

WEDNESDAY	THURSDAY	FRIDAY

Notes	MONDAY	TUESDAY

WEDNESDAY	THURSDAY	FRIDAY

Notes	MONDAY	TUESDAY

WEDNESDAY	THURSDAY	FRIDAY

Notes	MONDAY	TUESDAY

WEDNESDAY	THURSDAY	FRIDAY

Notes	MONDAY	TUESDAY

WEDNESDAY	THURSDAY	FRIDAY

WEEK OF

Notes	MONDAY	TUESDAY

WEDNESDAY	THURSDAY	FRIDAY

Notes	MONDAY	TUESDAY

WEDNESDAY	THURSDAY	FRIDAY

Notes	MONDAY	TUESDAY

WEDNESDAY	THURSDAY	FRIDAY

Notes

MONDAY

TUESDAY

WEDNESDAY	THURSDAY	FRIDAY

Notes

MONDAY

TUESDAY

WEDNESDAY	THURSDAY	FRIDAY

Notes	MONDAY	TUESDAY

WEDNESDAY	THURSDAY	FRIDAY

WEEK OF

Notes

MONDAY

TUESDAY

WEDNESDAY	THURSDAY	FRIDAY

◖◗ Notes ◖◗	MONDAY	TUESDAY

WEDNESDAY	THURSDAY	FRIDAY

Notes	MONDAY	TUESDAY

WEDNESDAY	THURSDAY	FRIDAY

WEEK OF

Notes	MONDAY	TUESDAY

WEDNESDAY	THURSDAY	FRIDAY

WEEK OF

Notes	MONDAY	TUESDAY

WEDNESDAY	THURSDAY	FRIDAY

Notes	MONDAY	TUESDAY

WEDNESDAY	THURSDAY	FRIDAY

Notes	MONDAY	TUESDAY

WEDNESDAY	THURSDAY	FRIDAY

Notes	MONDAY	TUESDAY

WEDNESDAY	THURSDAY	FRIDAY

Notes	MONDAY	TUESDAY

WEDNESDAY	THURSDAY	FRIDAY

Notes	MONDAY	TUESDAY

WEDNESDAY	THURSDAY	FRIDAY

Notes	MONDAY	TUESDAY

WEDNESDAY	THURSDAY	FRIDAY

Notes

MONDAY

TUESDAY

WEDNESDAY	THURSDAY	FRIDAY

Notes	MONDAY	TUESDAY

WEDNESDAY	THURSDAY	FRIDAY

GRADING CHART

Left axis: Total Number of Items (rows). Bottom axis: columns 1–30.

Items	1	2	3	4	5	6	7	8	9	10	11	12	13	14	15	16	17	18	19	20	21	22	23	24	25	26	27	28	29	30
50	98	96	94	92	90	88	86	84	82	80	78	76	74	72	70	68	66	64	62	60	58	56	54	52	50	48	46	44	42	
49	98	96	94	92	90	88	86	84	82	80	78	76	73	71	69	67	65	63	61	59	57	55	53	51	49	47	45	43	41	
48	98	96	94	92	90	88	85	83	81	79	77	75	73	71	69	67	65	63	60	58	56	54	52	50	48	46	44	42	40	
47	98	96	94	91	89	87	85	83	81	79	77	74	72	70	68	66	64	62	60	57	55	53	51	49	47	45	43	40	38	
46	98	96	93	91	89	87	85	81	80	78	76	74	72	70	67	65	63	61	59	57	54	52	50	48	46	43	41	39	37	
45	98	95	93	91	89	87	84	82	80	78	76	73	71	69	67	64	62	60	58	56	53	51	49	47	44	42	40	38	36	
44	98	95	93	91	89	86	84	82	80	77	75	73	70	68	66	64	61	59	57	55	52	50	48	45	43	41	39	36	34	
43	98	95	93	91	88	86	84	81	79	77	74	72	70	67	65	63	60	58	56	53	51	49	47	44	42	40	37	35	33	
42	98	95	93	90	88	86	83	81	79	76	74	71	69	67	64	62	60	57	55	52	50	48	45	43	40	38	36	33	31	
41	98	95	93	90	88	85	83	80	78	75	73	71	68	66	63	61	59	56	54	51	49	46	44	41	39	37	34	32	29	
40	98	95	93	90	88	85	83	80	78	75	73	70	68	65	63	60	58	55	53	50	48	45	43	40	38	35	33	30	28	
39	97	95	92	90	87	85	82	79	77	74	72	69	67	64	62	59	56	54	51	49	46	44	41	38	36	33	31	28	26	
38	97	95	92	89	87	84	82	79	76	74	71	68	66	63	61	58	55	53	50	47	45	42	39	37	34	32	29	26	24	
37	97	95	92	89	86	84	81	78	76	73	70	68	65	62	59	57	54	51	49	46	43	41	38	35	32	30	27	24	22	19
36	97	94	92	89	86	83	81	78	75	72	69	67	64	61	58	56	53	50	47	44	42	39	36	33	31	28	25	22	19	
35	97	94	91	89	86	83	80	77	74	71	69	66	63	60	57	54	51	49	46	43	40	37	34	31	29	26	23	20	17	
34	97	94	91	88	85	82	79	76	74	71	68	65	62	59	56	53	50	47	44	41	38	35	32	29	26	24	21	18	15	
33	97	94	91	88	85	82	79	76	73	70	67	64	61	58	55	52	48	45	42	39	36	33	30	27	24	21	18	15	12	
32	97	94	91	88	84	81	78	75	72	69	66	63	59	56	53	50	47	44	41	38	34	31	28	25	22	19	16	13	9	
31	97	94	90	87	84	81	77	74	71	68	65	61	58	55	52	48	45	42	39	35	32	29	26	23	19	16	13	10	6	
30	97	93	90	87	83	80	77	73	70	67	63	60	57	53	50	47	43	40	37	33	30	27	23	20	17	13	10	7	3	
29	97	93	90	86	83	79	76	72	69	66	62	59	55	52	48	45	41	38	34	31	28	24	21	17	14	10	7	3		
28	96	93	89	86	82	79	75	71	68	64	61	57	54	50	46	43	39	36	32	29	25	21	18	14	11	7	4			
27	96	93	89	85	81	78	74	70	67	63	59	56	52	48	44	41	37	33	30	26	22	19	15	11	7	4				
26	96	92	88	85	81	77	73	69	65	62	58	54	50	46	42	38	35	31	27	23	19	15	12	8	4					
25	96	92	88	84	80	76	72	68	64	60	56	52	48	44	40	36	32	28	24	20	16	12	8	4						
24	96	92	88	83	79	75	71	67	63	58	54	50	46	42	38	33	29	25	21	17	13	8	4							
23	96	91	87	83	78	74	70	65	61	57	52	48	43	39	35	30	26	22	17	13	9	4								
22	95	91	86	82	77	73	68	64	59	55	50	45	41	36	32	27	23	18	14	9	5									
21	95	90	86	81	76	71	67	62	57	52	48	43	38	33	29	24	19	14	10	5										
20	95	90	85	80	75	70	65	60	55	50	45	40	35	30	25	20	15	10	5											
19	95	89	84	79	74	68	63	58	53	47	42	37	32	26	21	16	11	5												
18	94	89	83	78	72	67	61	56	50	44	39	33	28	22	17	11	6													
17	94	88	82	76	71	65	59	53	47	41	35	29	24	19	12	6														
16	94	88	81	75	69	63	56	50	44	38	31	25	19	13	6															
15	93	87	80	73	67	60	53	47	40	33	27	20	13	7																
14	93	86	79	71	64	57	50	43	36	29	21	14	7																	
13	92	85	77	69	62	54	46	38	31	23	15	8																		
12	92	83	75	67	58	50	42	33	25	17	8																			
11	91	82	73	64	55	45	36	27	18	9																				
10	90	80	70	60	50	40	30	20	10																					
9	89	78	67	56	44	33	22	11																						
8	88	75	63	50	38	25	13																							
7	86	71	57	43	29	14																								
6	83	67	50	33	17																									
5	80	60	40	20																										
4	75	50	25																											
3	67	33																												